WORKBOOK

For

Fourteen Talks by Age Fourteen:

The Key Conversations You Must Have with Your Kids Before They Enter High School

Irene Franklin

Table of Contents

HOW TO USE THIS WORKBOOK

Welcome to the companion workbook to Michelle Icard's Fourteen Talks by Age Fourteen. This worksheet is intended to increase your engagement with the book's content and expand your awareness of the critical talks that must occur before your kid begins high school. It seeks to give practical skills for successful communication with your adolescent by summarizing major chapters, emphasizing key insights, presenting self-reflection questions, offering life-changing tasks, and prompting self-evaluations.

This workbook is designed as a complement to Fourteen Talks by Age Fourteen. It is not a replacement for the original material, but rather a tool to help you better understand and implement its concepts. Please use this worksheet in conjunction with the text to acquire a complete comprehension.

Guidelines for using the workbook:

- Chapter Summaries: Each chapter summary provides a concise review of the main ideas and insights explored in the preceding chapter in Fourteen Talks by Age Fourteen. Use these summaries to refresh your memory or rapidly review important points before beginning the workbook tasks.

- Important points: After studying each chapter summary, make a note of the important points that stand out to you. These insights will serve as a starting point for further discussion and application of the book's ideas in your interactions with your adolescent.

- Self-Reflection Questions: Following each set of chapter summaries, you will discover self-reflection questions intended to encourage introspection and a better understanding of your communication tactics and connection with your adolescent. Take some time to think about these questions, and consider writing down your answers for clarity.

- Life-Changing activities: The workbook offers a range of activities based on the teachings from Fourteen Talks by Age Fourteen. These activities are designed to help you incorporate the book's principles into your everyday interactions with your adolescent, promoting development, better communication, and a stronger parent-child connection. Choose workouts that appeal to you and include them into your regimen for real results.

- Self-Evaluation Questions: At the conclusion of the workbook, you'll discover self-evaluation questions to help you track your success and improvement as you apply the book's ideas. Use these questions to reflect on your accomplishments, identify areas for growth, and create objectives for future development in your relationship with your adolescent.

OVERVIEW

Michelle Icard's Fourteen Talks by Age Fourteen is a helpful resource for parents negotiating the sometimes difficult communication environment with their pre-teens and early teenagers. The book focuses on vital talks that parents should have with their children before they start high school, including subjects that are critical for their personal, emotional, and social growth. Icard, an adolescent development specialist, offers parents resources, techniques, and insights for approaching these critical conversations with empathy, openness, and clarity.

The book's basic premise is that when pre-teens enter puberty, they experience fast physical, emotional, and social development. Icard underlines that parents' communication with their children must grow as well. Rather of merely giving directions or advice, parents should encourage open talks that promote curiosity and comprehension. This is why the book starts with a section on preparing parents for these talks. In these early chapters, Icard assists parents in "learning a new language" of communication, one more suited to teenagers' developing demand for independence and self-expression. She also teaches tactics and cautions about potential "conversation crashers"—mistakes that often derail a teen's readiness to participate, such as overreacting or offering unwanted lectures.

The second section of the book delves into the fourteen crucial discussions that Icard feels parents should have with their children. These chats span a broad variety of themes, including independence, friendship, technology, and sexuality. Each chat includes practical tips for parents on when and how to bring up these issues. Icard advises parents to be proactive, rather than reactive, in these interactions, therefore fostering trust and understanding before difficulties or misunderstandings emerge.

For example, while discussing friendships, Icard describes how peer connections vary throughout puberty and how parents may help their children navigate these transformations without being too controlling. On the subject of technology, she accepts that children will inevitably get involved with social media and online platforms, but she also offers ways for encouraging responsible and thoughtful use. When addressing sexuality, Icard advises parents to approach the matter openly and without shame, so that their children feel knowledgeable and comfortable sharing any questions or concerns.

Throughout the book, Icard emphasizes the significance of combining supervision with respect for a child's developing independence. Rather than prescribing conduct, she supports for assisting youngsters in understanding the repercussions of their actions, whether they are dealing with money, criticism, or body image. The objective is to provide children with the emotional intelligence and resilience they need to navigate the world confidently.

One of the book's strong points is its practical approach. Each chapter contains advice, scripts, and examples to help parents design their talks. Icard highlights that these conversations do not have to be one-time, serious sit-downs, but can be seamlessly interwoven into everyday life, ensuring that children feel safe approaching their parents with questions or concerns.

CHAPTER 1: TIME TO LEARN A NEW LANGUAGE.

Chapter Summary:

In Chapter 1, Michelle Icard underlines the need of changing how parents connect with their children when they enter their adolescence. The conventional parent-child relationship shifts, as teenagers grow more autonomous, wanting to build their own identities. According to Icard, parents must change their communication style to fit their child's developing demand for autonomy and self-expression, much like learning a new language. She advises parents to concentrate on developing interactions that promote understanding and openness rather than offering clear directives. By learning to "speak teen," parents may create an atmosphere in which their children feel heard and encouraged while yet offering direction and limits. The chapter establishes the tone for the remainder of the book, giving parents a basis for comprehending the new issues of teenage communication.

Key Takeaways:

- Adolescents need a communication style that reflects their developing independence.

- Effective communication with teenagers entails listening more and speaking less.

- Instead of attempting to dominate interactions with teenagers, help them to make meaningful decisions.

- Communication throughout adolescence should emphasize transparency and trust.

- Teenagers want to be treated with respect and maturity, even when they make errors.

- Conversations that seem like lectures will alienate adolescents rather than draw them closer.

- Adapting your communication style to your teen's requirements leads to a stronger, more meaningful connection.

Self-Reflection Questions:

How are you presently communicating with your teen? Do you give them room to express themselves?

_____

_____

_____

_____

_____

_____

How can you change your communication approach to better meet your teen's demand for independence?

_____

_____

_____

_____

_____

Do you find yourself offering more advise or having more meaningful conversations with your teenager?

_____

_____

_____

_____

_____

_____

Are there times when your kid may feel as if you are speaking "at" them rather than "with" them?

_____

_____

_____

_____

_____

_____

How can you foster a feeling of openness and trust in your talks with your teenager?

_____

_____

_____

_____

_____

_____

How effectively do you listen to your adolescent without interrupting or attempting to answer their problems?

_____

_____

_____

_____

_____

_____

Life-Changing Exercises:

For one week, observe how you communicate with your adolescent, taking note of any times when you may dominate the discussion.

Active listening involves repeating what your adolescent says before adding your own perspective.

Allow your kid to make a tiny, low-stakes choice on their own and discuss the results together.

Ask open-ended inquiries about your teen's day or hobbies, enabling them to take the initiative.

When providing feedback, replace demands with recommendations and questions, including your adolescent in the discussion.

Play a challenging discussion with your adolescent, with each of you taking turns as the "parent" and "teen."

Write out three concrete instances where you can be more receptive to your teen's ideas or opinions.

Set aside time each week for an undisturbed, relaxed talk with your adolescent, keeping the emphasis on connection rather than correction.

CHAPTER TWO: YOUR NEW BAG OF TRICKS

Chapter Summary:

In this chapter, Michelle Icard discusses a range of tactics or "tricks" that parents may use to connect successfully with their teenagers. These tools are intended to enable open and fruitful discussions, especially about challenging issues. Icard emphasizes that parents should approach their conversations with empathy and tolerance, acknowledging that teenagers are in a developmental period when emotions might run high and reasoning may not always be at the forefront. She explains tactics such as properly timing interactions, providing safe places for debate, and utilizing comedy to relieve stress. The chapter advises parents to create a toolbox of communication skills that are appropriate for their parenting style and their child's temperament, stressing the need of flexibility and understanding. The idea is to create an atmosphere in which teenagers feel secure to express themselves, knowing that their parents would listen without judgment or overreaction.

Key Takeaways:

- Timing is critical; choosing the correct time for key interactions boosts their efficacy.
- Humor may be an effective strategy for reducing tension and making unpleasant talks more manageable.
- Teens react better when they see interactions as collaborative rather than antagonistic.
- Teenagers are more likely to open up and discuss their opinions in safe, nonjudgmental surroundings.
- Flexibility in your approach allows you to adjust to your teen's emotional condition and demands.
- Parents who maintain a calm, caring tone may help kids deal with their emotional outbursts.

- Small, regular attempts to engage with your adolescent may result in more meaningful and fruitful discussions.

Self-Reflection Questions:

Do you regularly select the proper time to have key talks with your teen?

_____

_____

_____

_____

_____

_____

How can you bring more fun and lightness to challenging conversations with your teen?

_____

_____

_____

_____

_____

_____

Are you adaptable in your communication style, or do you cling to one even when it isn't working?

_____

_____

_____

_____

_____

_____

Do you establish a secure atmosphere in which your adolescent feels comfortable expressing themselves without fear of being judged?

_____

_____

_____

_____

_____

_____

What ways can you demonstrate greater empathy when your adolescent is experiencing emotional difficulties?

_____

_____

_____

_____

_____

_____

How can you better regulate your own emotional reactions while having challenging talks with your teen?

_____

_____

_____

_____

_____

_____

Life-Changing Exercises:

Pay attention to your teen's mood and energy levels before starting key talks to ensure the moment is correct.

Use comedy the next time a discussion turns stressful, and see how it affects the dynamic.

Create a "judgment-free" zone at home where your adolescent can express themselves freely without fear of being judged.

Role-play a difficult discussion with another adult, exploring with various tones and approaches.

After a chat with your adolescent, consider what went well and what might have been done differently.

Plan a casual activity with your adolescent that encourages communication (e.g., a stroll or a drive), while keeping the environment light and open.

When your adolescent shows intense emotions, show empathy rather than react emotionally.

Keep a log of the numerous communication tactics you use with your adolescent, noting which ones seem to be the most beneficial.

CHAPTER THREE: CONVERSATION CRASHERS

Chapter Summary:

In Chapter 3, Icard discusses frequent "conversation crashers" that parents make while attempting to communicate with their children. These are habits that, although frequently unintended, may disrupt communication and cause dissatisfaction on both parties. Icard identifies various tendencies that might disrupt talks, including lecturing, interrupting, overreacting, and attempting to cure everything. She underlines that, although parents may have good intentions, their behaviors may make teenagers feel disregarded, condemned, or smothered, leading to disengagement. The chapter advises parents to be aware of their own communication patterns and to realize when they may be unintentionally impeding the discourse they are attempting to develop. By being more self-aware and avoiding these typical traps, parents may foster a more open and trustworthy relationship with their children.

Key Takeaways:

- Teenagers may get disengaged if they believe they are being lectured at.

- Interrupting your kid during a discussion indicates that their opinions and emotions are not appreciated.

- Overreacting to what your kid says may deter them from opening up in the future.

- Attempting to answer every issue your adolescent raises deprives them of the chance to think critically and solve it for themselves.

- Judging or condemning kids' thoughts or behaviors too fast undermines trust and transparency.

- Teens are more inclined to listen and participate in talks if they feel heard and appreciated.

- To avoid conversation crashers, you must be self-aware and motivated to adjust your entrenched communication behaviors.

Self-Reflection Questions:

Do you find yourself scolding your teenager instead of engaging in a two-way conversation?

_____

_____

_____

_____

_____

_____

How frequently do you interrupt your adolescent when they are talking? What message may that be conveying?

_____

_____

_____

_____

_____

_____

Do you tend to have strong reactions to your teen's comments or actions? How do you remain impartial in certain situations?

_____

_____

_____

_____

_____

_____

Do you ever attempt to fix issues for your adolescent instead of letting them sort things out on their own?

_____

_____

_____

_____

_____

_____

How can you show your adolescent that you appreciate their opinion, even if you disagree with it?

_____

_____

_____

_____

_____

_____

What communication patterns do you have that may be unwittingly cutting off interactions with your teen?

_____

_____

_____

_____

_____

_____

Life-Changing Exercises:

Practice listening to your adolescent without interrupting, even if you feel compelled to answer instantly.

Instead of lecturing your kid, stop and ask him or her an open-ended question.

When your kid discloses anything, avoid the desire to overreact; instead, remain cool and allow the discussion to run organically.

Allow your kid to solve a little issue on their own without presenting a solution, then debate their method later.

Review a previous discussion in which you may have rushed to criticize your teen's point of view, and consider how you may approach it better in the future.

For one week, concentrate on asking questions that encourage your adolescent to think critically rather than providing answers straight away.

Record and reflect on times when you saw yourself indulging in a "conversation crasher" behavior, and then discuss strategies to alter it.

Role-play with a partner or another adult to practice not lecturing, interrupting, or overreacting during a discussion.

CHAPTER 4: DISCUSSING YOUR PARENT-CHILD RELATIONSHIP.

Chapter Summary:

This chapter highlights the necessity of addressing the parent-child connection, which serves as the basis for trust and mutual respect. Icard urges parents to communicate honestly with their children about how their connection is changing as the kid grows. Rather of hanging onto childhood patterns, parents should recognize that their kid is growing more autonomous and capable of making choices. This discussion is about recalibrating the connection to fit the needs of both the parent and the adolescent, ensuring that it remains a source of support and direction while not becoming suffocating or dominating. Icard emphasizes the need of honesty, openness, and a willingness to discuss limits and expectations as the kid matures.

Key Takeaways:

- Discussing the dynamic parent-child connection promotes mutual understanding and respect.

- Recognizing your teen's increasing independence demonstrates that you value their autonomy.

- Open discussions about expectations reduce misunderstandings and anger.

- Teens need to be heard and appreciated as they form their identities.

- Boundaries and regulations should be fluid and renegotiated as your kid grows.

- Honest conversations about your own emotions and expectations create a good model for your teenager.

- As the adolescent becomes more independent, the parent-child connection should shift from control to guiding.

Self-Reflection Questions:

How has your connection with your adolescent altered as they've become older? Have you acknowledged these changes?

_____

_____

_____

_____

_____

_____

Do you freely express your expectations with your teenager, and do they feel comfortable sharing theirs with you?

_____

_____

_____

_____

_____

_____

How can you better accept your teen's developing desire for independence while yet offering guidance?

_____

_____

_____

_____

_____

_____

In what ways do you show your love and support for your adolescent, particularly as they want greater independence?

_____

_____

_____

_____

_____

_____

Are there any limits or regulations that may be adjusted to better suit your teen's current stage of development?

_____

_____

_____

_____

_____

How well do you combine being a parent and giving your adolescent freedom to make their own decisions?

_____

_____

_____

_____

_____

Life-Changing Exercises:

Sit down with your adolescent and talk openly about how your relationship has changed and how it can continue to improve.

Ask your adolescent how they feel about the present rules and limits in place, and talk about any possible changes.

Write out three ways you may offer your adolescent greater respect for their independence in daily situations.

The next time your adolescent expresses opinions or sentiments regarding your relationship, engage in active listening.

Consider your own expectations for your adolescent and if they are consistent with the person they are becoming.

Set up a "relationship check-in" ritual in which you and your adolescent discuss how things are going and what may be improved.

Identify situations when you may be clinging onto old dynamics from their upbringing and intentionally release them.

Set aside time each week to do something that enhances your relationship, such as a common hobby or passion.

CHAPTER 5: TALKING ABOUT INDEPENDENCE

Chapter Summary:

In Chapter 5, Michelle Icard discusses the crucial debate over independence. Adolescence is a time when youngsters begin to establish their individuality, and Icard emphasizes that this desire for independence is a natural and important aspect of growing up. However, it may frequently be difficult for parents who struggle with letting go of control. Icard offers advice on how to manage this transition, assisting parents in supporting their teen's need for independence but also offering a foundation of safety and direction. She emphasizes the need of instilling responsibility and accountability in teenagers, enabling them to make choices and learn from their errors in a low-risk setting. This discussion is about progressively passing up authority in a manner that allows kids to mature into effective and responsible adults without jeopardizing their safety or well-being.

Key Takeaways:

- Adolescence is a natural period for teenagers to express their independence, and parents should encourage this development.

- Granting independence does not imply relinquishing all control; rather, it is about balancing freedom and responsibility.

- Teens need chances to make choices and face consequences in a safe, controlled setting.

- Allowing teenagers to accept responsibility for their decisions promotes self-reliance and accountability.

- Independence is a continuous process that requires open communication and trust.

- Parents should stop micromanaging their teen's lives and instead provide direction and assistance as required.

- The purpose of offering freedom is to assist teenagers gain confidence in their abilities to navigate the world alone.

Self-Reflection Questions:

How comfortable are you with giving your adolescent greater independence? Do you struggle to let go of control?

_____

_____

_____

_____

_____

_____

Are you giving your adolescent opportunity to make their own choices and learn from the consequences?

_____

_____

_____

_____

_____

_____

How do you strike a balance between providing direction and allowing your teen to sort things out on their own?

_____

_____

_____

_____

_____

_____

In what ways do you help your adolescent develop a feeling of duty and accountability?

_____

_____

_____

_____

_____

_____

Are you creating an atmosphere in which your adolescent feels secure making errors and learning from them?

_____

_____

_____

_____

_____

_____

How can you model healthy independence in your own life so that your adolescent might learn from it?

_____

_____

_____

_____

_____

_____

Life-Changing Exercises:

Determine one aspect of your teen's life in which you can offer them greater control, such as controlling their own schedule or making choices about their activities.

Talk to your adolescent about what independence means to them and when they feel ready for additional responsibilities.

Create a "decision journal" in which your adolescent may record their decisions and reflect on the results.

Allow your adolescent to organize and carry out a family activity from start to end, and give them complete responsibility for the outcome.

Step aside during a little argument or problem and let your adolescent work through it alone.

Set up a family meeting to discuss and negotiate obligations and freedoms, giving your adolescent a say in the process.

Reflect on your own experiences with independence as a teen and share them with your kid.

When your kid tackles a crisis on their own, congratulate and support them, reinforcing their developing feeling of competence.

CHAPTER 6: DISCUSSING CHANGING FRIENDSHIPS.

Chapter Summary:

In Chapter 6, Icard explains how friendships might become more problematic throughout adolescence. Teens are discovering out who they are, thus their friendships may fluctuate or change radically. Icard emphasizes how these changing social dynamics may be difficult for both teenagers and their parents, particularly when friendships expire or disagreement emerges. She advises parents to have open conversations with their teenagers about the fluid nature of friendships, so that they realize that change is a natural aspect of life. Icard also advises parents on how to help their teenagers navigate disagreements and emotional upheaval that typically accompany changing social groups. The purpose of this talk is to help kids negotiate friendships with confidence and resilience, giving them the skills they need to maintain good relationships and deal with the inevitable changes that occur with growing up.

Key Takeaways:

- Friendships throughout adolescence are often changeable, and kids need help as they negotiate these changes.

- It is important for teenagers to recognize that friendship changes are a natural aspect of growing up.

- Conflicts in friendships may teach significant lessons about communication, empathy, and conflict resolution.

- Parents should not attempt to regulate their teen's social life, but rather help them create good connections.

- Helping kids deal with the emotional ups and downs of friendships increases emotional intelligence and resilience.

- Healthy friendships are built on mutual respect, trust, and shared ideals, and teenagers must identify when a connection is no longer beneficial.
- Navigating shifting alliances helps teenagers build social skills that will benefit them throughout their lives.

Self-Reflection Questions:

How do you now help your adolescent navigate friendship changes? Are you engaged or distant?

_____

_____

_____

_____

_____

_____

Are you creating a secure environment for your adolescent to vent their emotions regarding disputes or changes in their social circle?

_____

_____

_____

_____

_____

_____

How can you help your child navigate the emotional problems of friendship transitions without asserting control?

_____

_____

_____

_____

_____

_____

What principles do you want your adolescent to emphasize in their friendships? How do you help them identify these?

_____

_____

_____

_____

_____

_____

How successfully do you model healthy friendships for your teen?

_____

_____

_____

_____

_____

_____

How can you help your adolescent to manage relationship issues with maturity and empathy?

_____

_____

_____

_____

_____

_____

Life-Changing Exercises:

Talk to your kid about the friendships they value and why, and help them think on what makes a connection beneficial or bad.

Encourage your kid to contact a buddy they haven't talked with in a while to help them reconnect and handle shifting circumstances.

Role-play a conflict resolution scenario with your adolescent to help them learn how to manage arguments with peers.

Make a gratitude list with your adolescent, focusing on the excellent friendships in their lives and the lessons they've gained from them.

Discuss with your kid the necessity of relationship boundaries and how to establish them appropriately.

Encourage your adolescent to keep a diary on their friendships, focusing on how they have developed and evolved over time.

Create a family conversation about the characteristics of good relationships and friendships, using examples from your own experience.

Plan a social gathering where your adolescent may bring friends over and establish friendships in a secure, supportive setting.

CHAPTER 7: TALKING ABOUT CREATIVITY

Chapter Summary:

In Chapter 7, Michelle Icard explores the often-overlooked topic of creativity. Adolescence is a period when teenagers begin to discover their interests, hobbies, and abilities, and creativity plays an important part in this process. Icard urges parents to promote their teenagers' creative pursuits, whether via painting, music, writing, or problem solving. Creativity is more than just creative expression; it is also about encouraging inventive thinking and enabling teenagers to explore with new ideas and viewpoints. Icard emphasizes that parents should promote discovery and avoid imposing limits or expectations on what creativity should look like. By having open talks about creativity, parents can help their teenagers explore their hobbies, gain confidence, and establish a worldview that values innovation and curiosity.

Key Takeaways:

- Creativity is vital for personal development and allows kids to explore their hobbies and interests.

- Supporting your teenager's artistic endeavors fosters self-expression and confidence.

- Creativity is not confined to the arts; it also encompasses problem solving, invention, and fresh ways of thinking.

- Teens need the flexibility to explore various creative avenues without being pressured or held to unrealistic standards.

- Encouraging creativity helps kids build critical thinking skills and resilience as they learn to accept failure and iterate.

- Conversations about creativity should emphasize inquiry and curiosity rather than success or production.

- Fostering creativity in adolescents supports long-term cognitive and emotional development.

Self-Reflection Questions:

How are you presently supporting or encouraging your teen's creativity? Could you do more to encourage this element of their development?

_____

_____

_____

_____

_____

_____

In what ways can you provide your adolescent greater opportunity to pursue their artistic interests?

_____

_____

_____

_____

_____

_____

Are there occasions when you may put your own standards on your teen's artistic endeavors?

_____

_____

_____

_____

_____

_____

How do you foster an atmosphere that encourages inquiry, creativity, and creative thinking?

_____

_____

_____

_____

_____

_____

What creative activities did you love as a teen, and how can you share them with your child?

_____

_____

_____

_____

_____

_____

How successfully do you accept failure and experimentation in your own life, demonstrating creative resilience to your teen?

_____

_____

_____

_____

_____

_____

Life-Changing Exercises:

Encourage your adolescent to start a new creative interest or experiment with a new form of artistic expression.

Have a brainstorming session with your adolescent about how to creatively tackle a real-world issue, with an emphasis on inventive thinking.

Attend a local art exhibit, concert, or cultural event with your adolescent to introduce them to different ways of being creative and expressive.

Set aside time for a family "creativity night" in which everyone participates in a creative activity of their choosing, such as sketching, writing, or constructing.

Tell your kid about a moment when you failed at something creative and what you learnt from it, encouraging them to accept failure as part of the process.

Encourage your adolescent to create a creative notebook in which they may scribble down ideas, drawings, or thoughts without being judged.

Consider doing a creative activity with your adolescent, such as cooking a new meal, creating something, or producing music.

Help your kid create a vision board with their creative aims and dreams, enabling them to dream and prepare for the future.

CHAPTER 8: TALKING ABOUT SELF-CARE

Chapter Summary:

Chapter 8 emphasizes the need of educating teenagers how to take care of themselves, both physically and psychologically. Icard highlights that adolescence is an important period to build self-care behaviors that will promote long-term health and well-being. Parents should encourage their teenagers to prioritize sleep, diet, exercise, and emotional well-being while also modeling these habits for themselves. The chapter illustrates that self-care is more than simply following routines; it also includes recognizing the importance of establishing boundaries, managing stress, and taking time to recover. Icard recommends having open discussions regarding the difficulties kids encounter in juggling school, social life, and personal time, which will help them identify when they are pushing themselves too hard. The ultimate objective is to help kids develop a strong sense of self-awareness, which will enable them to care for their bodies and brains in a manner that promotes long-term health and happiness.

Key Takeaways:

- Self-care is vital for physical and mental well-being and should be addressed beginning in adolescence.

- Teens want assistance on how to manage their time and energy while juggling school, social activities, and personal care.

- Good self-care practices begin with getting enough sleep, eating well, and exercising.

- Teaching teenagers how to detect the indications of stress or burnout is critical for avoiding long-term mental distress.

- Parents should model positive self-care activities and emphasize the value of leading a balanced lifestyle.

- Self-care also entails establishing boundaries, saying no when necessary, and taking time to rest.

- Open discussions on self-care empower teenagers to be aware of their own needs and to seek assistance when overwhelmed.

Self-Reflection Questions:

How do you now urge your adolescent to care for themselves physically and mentally?

_____

_____

_____

_____

_____

Are you modeling good self-care behaviors for your adolescent, or might you do better in this area?

_____

_____

_____

_____

_____

_____

What methods can you help your adolescent manage stress and balance their commitments?

_____

_____

_____

_____

_____

_____

Do you routinely address the benefits of rest, diet, and exercise with your teen?

_____

_____

_____

_____

_____

_____

How do you foster a family climate that values well-being and emotional health?

_____

_____

_____

_____

_____

_____

Are there any areas where your kid may be ignoring self-care, and how can you address them without being overbearing?

_____

_____

_____

_____

_____

_____

Life-Changing Exercises:

Make a weekly self-care schedule with your adolescent that includes time for sleep, exercise, relaxation, and nutritious foods.

Encourage your teenager to create a self-care notebook in which they may record how they feel physically and emotionally throughout the week.

Plan a "self-care day" for your family, with each member focusing on activities that promote relaxation and well-being.

Discuss the notion of "burnout" with your adolescent and help them detect indicators of it in their own lives, as well as provide prevention techniques.

Model boundary-setting by telling your adolescent about a moment when you had to say no to something for your own well-being, and urge them to follow suit.

Investigate mindfulness or relaxation practices with your adolescent, such as meditation, deep breathing, or yoga.

Discuss with your kid how they feel about their present academic and social burden, and explore strategies to alleviate unneeded stress.

Encourage your kid to arrange regular leisure throughout the week, stressing the value of rest and relaxation for long-term health.

CHAPTER 9: TALKING ABOUT FAIRNESS

Chapter Summary:

In Chapter 9, Icard discusses fairness, which is a common worry for teenagers as they negotiate the intricacies of social interactions, home life, and school settings. Teens are particularly sensitive to perceived injustices, and they may exhibit displeasure when they believe they are being treated unjustly or when they see unfairness in the world around them. Icard advises parents to have open talks about what fairness entails and to recognize that life is not always equitable. She argues that, although fairness is a good goal, it is important for teenagers to recognize that it is not always achievable, and they must learn how to cope with and react to unjust events. This chapter emphasizes the significance of instilling empathy in adolescents, educating them to advocate for themselves and others, and assisting them in developing a balanced view on fairness and justice.

Key Takeaways:

- Fairness is an important problem for teenagers, and they need assistance in comprehending its complexities and limits.

- Open discussions on justice allow teenagers to balance their idealistic and realistic viewpoints on life.

- Life is not always fair, and learning to deal with this truth fosters resilience and emotional maturity.

- Teenagers should be encouraged to speak out for themselves and others when they see injustice.

- It is critical for parents to respect their teen's views of justice, even when the circumstance cannot be altered.

- Empathy and compassion should be fostered alongside debates about justice, enabling them to consider the perspectives of others.

- Helping youth comprehend fairness as a notion that extends beyond personal concerns promotes a stronger sense of societal responsibility.

Self-Reflection Questions:

How do you react when your adolescent raises concerns about justice, either in their own life or in the society around them?

_____

_____

_____

_____

_____

_____

Are you educating your adolescent that, although fairness is an important ideal, it is not always possible?

_____

_____

_____

_____

_____

_____

How can you assist your adolescent develop empathy, compassion, and a desire for fairness?

_____

_____

_____

_____

_____

How do you exemplify fairness and justice in your personal relationships, with your adolescent and others?

_____

_____

_____

_____

_____

_____

How well do you strike a balance between acknowledging your teen's frustrations and helping them develop resilience to deal with unfairness?

_____

_____

_____

_____

_____

_____

What chances do you provide your adolescent to speak for themselves or others in circumstances when fairness is questioned?

_____

_____

_____

_____

_____

_____

Life-Changing Exercises:

Have a conversation with your kid about a recent scenario in which they thought things were unfair, and ask how they addressed it.

Encourage your adolescent to explore a fairness or justice topic that is important to them, and help them discover methods to become involved.

Role-play a situation in which your kid feels mistreated or treated unjustly, and walk them through how to advocate for themselves calmly and successfully.

Plan a family conversation about fairness, in which everyone shares their perspectives and experiences.

Explore historical or current events tales that emphasize concerns of fairness and justice, and talk about them with your adolescent.

Encourage your kid to develop empathy by thinking about a moment when they benefited from an unjust circumstance and how they may use that knowledge to assist others.

Create a "fairness challenge" in which your kid actively seeks ways to treat people fairly in their everyday encounters and keeps a record of their findings.

Help your child recognize an unjust issue at school or in their community, and then explore methods to remedy it.

CHAPTER 10: TALKING ABOUT TECHNOLOGY

Chapter Summary:

Chapter 10 explores how technology affects the lives of teenagers. Icard understands that technology, such as cellphones, social media, and the internet, plays an important part in contemporary adolescence, and she encourages parents to approach this discussion with an appreciation of both the advantages and problems that technology presents. The chapter delves into topics such as screen usage, cyberbullying, social comparison, and the pressure to maintain an active online presence. Icard urges parents to establish realistic limits while simultaneously enabling their teenagers to make responsible choices regarding technology usage. She highlights the necessity for open discussion, where parents and kids address not just rules and limits but also the emotional and social repercussions of living in a digital environment. Finally, the discussion regarding technology should be on instilling good habits and ensuring that technology is utilized as a tool rather than a cause of stress or injury.

Key Takeaways:

- Technology is an important element of teenagers' life, and parents should approach the topic with understanding rather than dread.

- Setting sensible limits on digital usage is vital, but kids must also learn to self-regulate.

- Open discussion about technology helps teenagers comprehend both its advantages and possible drawbacks.

- Cyberbullying, social comparison, and online pressure must all be handled with honesty and empathy.

- Teens should be encouraged to take breaks from technology to maintain a healthy balance between their online and offline lives.

- Parents could serve as role models for safe technology usage by exhibiting healthy practices in their own digital connections.
- The objective is to help teenagers build a sensible, balanced relationship with technology that enriches rather than detracts from their experiences.

Self-Reflection Questions:

How do you now communicate with your adolescent about technology? Are your talks centered on rules or understanding?

_____

_____

_____

_____

_____

_____

How can you assist your adolescent adopt healthy digital habits?

_____

_____

_____

_____

_____

_____

Do you provide a good example for your adolescent in terms of safe digital usage, or could you improve?

_____

_____

_____

_____

_____

How well do you deal with the emotional and social obstacles that technology presents, such as online pressure or social media comparison?

_____

_____

_____

_____

_____

_____

Are there any places where you might give your kid greater responsibility for managing their own digital use?

_____

_____

_____

_____

_____

_____

How can you strike a better balance between establishing limits and providing your adolescent autonomy in their digital life?

_____

_____

_____

_____

_____

_____

Life-Changing Exercises:

Hold a family gathering to review each member's technology use patterns, concerns, and suggestions for change.

Plan a "tech-free" day or evening in which the whole family disconnects from screens and spends time together offline.

Encourage your teenager to think about how they feel after using social media, noting both good and bad feelings.

Discuss with your kid the notion of "digital minimalism," and challenge them to limit their screen use for one week.

Role-play a scenario in which your adolescent is subjected to cyberbullying or online pressure, allowing them to practice responding correctly.

Create a family technology contract that sets realistic device use guidelines and expectations while allowing for flexibility and trust.

Encourage your adolescent to try establishing limits for their own technology usage, such as restricting alerts or scheduling screen breaks.

Explore alternate activities with your adolescent that encourage offline involvement, such as reading, hiking, or exercising a non-screen-related passion.

CHAPTER 11: TALKING ABOUT

CRITICISM

Chapter Summary:

In Chapter 11, Icard delves into the subject of criticism, which is an important problem for teenagers who are frequently sensitive to the views of others. Criticism may come from a variety of sources, including parents, instructors, classmates, and even oneself, and learning to take it constructively is an important ability. According to Icard, although some criticism might be harsh or unjust, it can also be used for development if handled appropriately. She advises parents to assist their teenagers in distinguishing between helpful and harmful criticism and teaching them to reflect on input rather than taking it personally. This chapter also focuses on helping teenagers build resilience in the face of negative criticism so that they may learn from it rather than get disheartened. Teens who see criticism as an opportunity for learning might develop a better attitude toward feedback and a higher sense of self-worth.

Key Takeaways:

- Criticism, while constructive, is a great tool for development, and kids must learn how to deal with it.

- Teens often take criticism personally, so parents should help them develop resilience in the face of unfavorable comments.

- It's critical to distinguish between constructive criticism, which is intended to assist, and destructive criticism, which is often damaging.

- Open discussions regarding criticism assist kids to think on feedback and utilize it to improve, rather than allowing it to lower their self-esteem.

- Teaching teenagers how to distinguish their self-worth from external criticism promotes confidence and emotional maturity.

- Teens should learn how to handle criticism from various persons in their life.

- Parents should show their children how to offer and take criticism graciously, emphasizing that it may be a learning opportunity.

Self-Reflection Questions:

How do you generally react to criticism, and how does your adolescent see you handling it?

_____

_____

_____

_____

_____

Are you teaching your adolescent the difference between helpful and harmful criticism?

_____

_____

_____

_____

_____

How can you help your adolescent handle negative comments without damaging their self-esteem?

_____

_____

_____

_____

_____

How can you teach your adolescent to see criticism as an opportunity for development rather than a personal attack?

_____

_____

_____

_____

_____

_____

Do you demonstrate good feedback and constructive criticism in your connection with your teen?

_____

_____

_____

_____

_____

_____

How can you help your adolescent acquire the strength to deal with criticism in a healthy and constructive way?

_____

_____

_____

_____

_____

_____

Life-Changing Exercises:

Have a chat with your kid about the most recent item of criticism they got, assisting them in reflecting on its worth and how to apply it for personal development.

Encourage your kid to start a "criticism journal" in which they monitor feedback and their emotional reactions while learning to handle it productively.

Play out a situation in which your adolescent gets severe criticism, and guide them on how to react calmly and wisely.

Practice providing constructive criticism to your adolescent in a supportive manner, asking them how they feel, and clarifying how feedback may help them improve.

Encourage your kid to offer themselves positive comments on a project or work they've finished, since this promotes self-reflection and progress.

Hold a family conversation about how each member manages criticism, including personal experiences and suggestions for handling feedback in a healthy manner.

Explore examples of prominent personalities or role models who have handled criticism graciously, and talk about what your adolescent can learn from their approach.

Create a feedback loop with your adolescent in which you both provide and receive constructive criticism on a project or joint work to practice mutual improvement.

CHAPTER 12: TALKING ABOUT HARD WORK

Chapter Summary:

Chapter 12 explores the topic of hard work and how parents may build a strong work ethic in their teenagers. Icard underlines that, although teenagers may avoid effort in favor of rapid pleasure, understanding the value of hard work is critical for long-term success and personal fulfillment. She advises parents to assist their teenagers in setting meaningful objectives and understanding the relationship between effort and accomplishment. This chapter emphasizes the value of perseverance, patience, and resilience, teaching youngsters that success is often the product of hard work rather than innate skill. Icard recommends parents to reward hard work rather than merely results, and to encourage teenagers to be proud of their achievements. Teens may learn to value the process of working toward their objectives by cultivating a growth mindset in which hard effort is seen as a means of development.

Key Takeaways:

- Hard work is a crucial life skill, and teenagers want direction on how to cultivate a strong work ethic.

- When it comes to accomplishment, effort and endurance sometimes outweigh inherent skill.

- Teens should be taught to create significant objectives and recognize that reaching them takes persistent work over time.

- Celebrating hard work rather than merely outcomes encourages teenagers to adopt a development attitude and take pleasure in their achievements.

- Failure is an unavoidable part of the process, and kids should understand that perseverance in the face of adversity leads to achievement.

- Teaching youth to appreciate the process of achieving their objectives promotes long-term resilience and happiness.

- Parents should demonstrate the importance of hard work in their own life, showing that effort leads to success.

Self-Reflection Questions:

How do you now teach your adolescent the importance of hard work and perseverance?

_____

_____

_____

_____

_____

_____

Are you appreciating your teen's efforts or are you more concerned with the results they achieve?

_____

_____

_____

_____

_____

_____

How can you inspire your adolescent to develop significant objectives and work consistently toward them?

_____

_____

_____

_____

_____

_____

Do you model the value of hard work in your own life, and how does your adolescent see it?

_____

_____

_____

_____

_____

_____

How can you assist your adolescent create a development mentality, where they realize that work leads to progress?

_____

_____

_____

_____

_____

_____

How can you assist your kid deal with setbacks and disappointments, and how can you encourage them to be more resilient?

_____

_____

_____

_____

_____

_____

Life-Changing Exercises:

Encourage your adolescent to select a long-term goal and break it down into smaller, more doable stages, rewarding their accomplishments along the way.

Discuss the value of hard work with your kid by sharing personal experiences where effort resulted in success.

Encourage your adolescent to think on a moment when they worked hard for something and succeeded, emphasizing the importance of perseverance.

Create a "hard work challenge" in which your adolescent picks a goal that will take consistent effort over a week or month and tracks their progress.

Play out a situation in which your kid has a setback or failure, and assist them in determining how to persevere in the face of adversity.

Watch a video or read about a person who attained success through hard effort, and explore what your adolescent can learn from their experience.

Encourage your kid to volunteer for an activity or project that needs persistent effort, so they may learn the value of hard work firsthand.

Set up a family conversation about the relationship between effort and accomplishment, in which everyone shares experiences of occasions when they worked hard to attain a goal.

CHAPTER 13: TALKING ABOUT MONEY

Chapter Summary:

Chapter 13 covers money and financial literacy, a key issue that many youths lack understanding about. Icard emphasizes the significance of educating teenagers how to handle their money appropriately, including budgeting, saving, and making sound financial choices. She argues that learning about money at a young age prepares teenagers for independence and adulthood, providing them with the skills they need to avoid debt and financial hardship. This chapter encourages parents to have open discussions about family finances, model excellent money management behaviors, and enable teenagers to experience managing money in low-risk scenarios. Icard advises parents to assist their teenagers have a healthy relationship with money, considering it as a tool for stability and opportunity rather than a cause of worry or dread.

Key Takeaways:

- Financial literacy is critical for teenagers as they prepare for independence, and parents should begin teaching money management early.

- Teens must learn how to budget, save, and make sound financial choices in order to prevent future debt or financial difficulty.

- Open discussions about family finances help kids understand money and learn how to handle it appropriately.

- Allowing youth to practice money management in low-risk scenarios, such as allowances or part-time work, boosts confidence.

- Teens should recognize the need of saving for both short- and long-term objectives, as well as living within their means.

- Parents should model good financial habits by planning, saving, and spending sensibly.

- Financial literacy teaches teenagers to see money as a tool for stability and opportunity, not as a cause of worry or dread.

Self-Reflection Questions:

How are you now teaching your teenager about money management and financial responsibility?

_____

_____

_____

_____

_____

Are you modeling good financial practices for your adolescent, or might you do more in this area?

_____

_____

_____

_____

_____

_____

How can you engage your adolescent in family financial talks while teaching them about budgeting and planning?

_____

_____

_____

_____

_____

_____

Do you provide your adolescent opportunity to practice money management, such as an allowance or a part-time job?

_____

_____

_____

_____

_____

_____

How can you assist your kid establish a balanced attitude to money, understanding the need of saving and spending wisely?

_____

_____

_____

_____

_____

How are you training your adolescent for financial independence as they approach adulthood?

_____

_____

_____

_____

_____

_____

Life-Changing Exercises:

Sit down with your adolescent and make a basic budget for their allowance or wages, teaching them how to manage funds for various needs and desires.

Encourage your kid to choose a financial goal, such as saving for a specific item, and assist them in developing a savings strategy to attain it.

Talk openly with your adolescent about the family budget, describing how you manage household spending and save for the future.

Give your adolescent responsibility for a modest household cost for a month, such as grocery shopping on a budget, and evaluate their experience.

Help your kid start a savings account or introduce them to basic investing principles, demonstrating how they may increase their money over time.

Encourage your kid to study the cost of living in other cities or nations, which can help them grasp the value of budgeting for independence.

Role-play a situation in which your adolescent must make a difficult financial decision, addressing the trade-offs and repercussions of each option.

Set up a family financial challenge in which each member sets a monthly financial objective, such as saving, spending less, or keeping to a budget.

CHAPTER 14: TALKING ABOUT SEXUALITY

Chapter Summary:

Chapter 14 addresses the difficult issue of sexuality, providing youth with factual information and assistance in a courteous and open way. Icard highlights the need of continual sexuality talks, which should include subjects such as sexual health, consent, partnerships, and personal beliefs. The chapter emphasizes the significance of providing a secure environment in which youth may ask questions and share their concerns without fear of repercussions. Icard urges parents to approach these talks with transparency and kindness, ensuring that their teenagers have access to accurate information and assistance. Parents may assist their teenagers make responsible choices and build a healthy awareness of their own sexuality by discussing it thoughtfully and intelligently.

Key Takeaways:

- Conversations about sexuality should continue, providing youth with continuing support and knowledge as they mature.

- It is critical to provide a secure, nonjudgmental atmosphere in which youth feel comfortable addressing sexual health and associated topics.

- Accurate knowledge on sexual health, consent, and relationships enables teenagers to make educated and responsible choices.

- Parents should explain sexuality with openness and sensitivity, including both factual and emotional elements.

- Encourage teenagers to ask questions and voice their concerns so that they feel supported and understood.

- Providing trustworthy materials and assistance empowers teenagers to handle their sexuality ethically and healthfully.

- Addressing personal sexual ideals and expectations helps teenagers make choices that are consistent with their own views and standards.

Self-Reflection Questions:

How comfortable are you talking sexuality with your teenager, and how can you improve in this area?

_____

_____

_____

_____

_____

_____

Do you provide your adolescent accurate and complete information on sexual health and relationships?

_____

_____

_____

_____

_____

How can you provide a secure environment for your adolescent to ask questions and voice concerns about sexuality?

_____

_____

_____

_____

_____

_____

Are you willing to communicate your own sexual principles and ideas while also appreciating your teen's point of view?

_____

_____

_____

_____

_____

_____

How do you guarantee that your sexuality talks are continuous and include both factual and emotive topics?

_____

_____

_____

_____

_____

_____

How can you help your adolescent make educated and responsible choices regarding their sexuality?

_____

_____

_____

_____

_____

_____

Life-Changing Exercises:

Have an open and honest conversation with your adolescent about a recent news article or current event involving sexuality, examining many points of view and facts.

Make a list of reputable sources (websites, books, and specialists) that give accurate sexual health information and share it with your adolescent.

Role-play a situation in which your adolescent must make a decision about their sexuality, allowing them to examine their beliefs and options.

Schedule frequent "check-in" talks with your adolescent about their knowledge of sexuality and relationships, and provide support and direction as necessary.

Encourage your adolescent to write down their thoughts and questions regarding sexuality in a notebook, and then go over them together to clarify any worries or misunderstandings.

Invite a trustworthy expert, such as a sexual health educator, to meet with your adolescent and answer their concerns in a safe and educational environment.

Discuss the notion of consent and healthy relationships with your adolescent, using real-life examples to highlight crucial concepts and limits.

Examine your own sexual ideals and views, and evaluate how they affect your talks with your adolescent, establishing a mix of instruction and respect for their individuality.

CHAPTER 15: DISCUSSING REPUTATIONS

Chapter Summary:

Chapter 15 delves into the topic of reputation and its relevance in a teen's life. Icard describes how teenagers are acutely aware of their social image and how it might affect their self-esteem and relationships. The chapter emphasizes the necessity of realizing that, although reputations may be impacted by others, they must be founded on genuine conduct and ideals. Icard advises parents to assist their adolescents build a strong reputation by emphasizing honesty, compassion, and respect above seeking praise or fitting in. The chapter also discusses the possible consequences of being too concerned about one's reputation, such as surrendering one's principles or indulging in undesirable actions in order to obtain approval. Parents may assist their teenagers in developing a reputation that represents their genuine nature by supporting honest self-expression and self-awareness.

Key Takeaways:

- Teens appreciate reputation, but it should be founded on honesty and own ideals, not external acceptance.

- Teens should be taught to behave with honesty, compassion, and respect, since this will help them establish a good reputation.

- Teens who understand that their reputation may be impacted but should not govern their conduct are more likely to preserve self-esteem and sincerity.

- Being too concerned about reputation might lead to undesirable conduct or surrendering one's ideals in order to fit in.

- Open talks about how reputation affects relationships and self-esteem may help teenagers deal with societal pressures.

- Parents should demonstrate how to establish and maintain a good reputation via their own activities and relationships.

- Encourage kids to concentrate on their own beliefs and aspirations rather than seeking external approval, which promotes real self-confidence.

Self-Reflection Questions:

How can you explain to your adolescent the significance of reputation and how it connects to their values and behavior?

_____

_____

_____

_____

_____

_____

Are you teaching your adolescent the distinction between real self-expression and seeking acceptance from others?

_____

_____

_____

_____

_____

_____

How can you help your kid develop a good reputation based on honesty and kindness?

_____

_____

_____

_____

_____

_____

Do you model a good reputation via your own conduct, and how does this impact your teen's perception of reputation?

_____

_____

_____

_____

_____

_____

How can you assist your kid strike a balance between their worry about their reputation and their own values?

_____

_____

_____

_____

_____

_____

How can you help your kid handle societal demands while being honest and self-respectful?

_____

_____

_____

_____

_____

_____

Life-Changing Exercises:

Discuss with your adolescent a moment when their actions had an impact on their reputation, including the consequences and lessons learned.

Encourage your kid to consider their basic principles and how they want these ideals to manifest in their actions and reputation.

Role-play situations in which your adolescent is pressured to behave against their ideals, allowing them to practice being true to themselves.

Create a family values statement outlining the concepts you feel are critical to establishing a great reputation, and address how each member can support these beliefs.

Encourage your kid to think on someone they like for their good reputation and assess what attributes or actions lead to that reputation.

Set up a "reputation challenge" in which your kid concentrates on acts of kindness or integrity for a week and then discusses how these activities affect their self-esteem.

Encourage your adolescent to compose a letter to themselves about their desired reputation and the measures they will take to attain it, and then review it together.

Discuss the notion of online reputation with your adolescent, including how their digital imprint affects their real-life reputation and promoting appropriate online conduct.

CHAPTER 16: DISCUSSING IMPULSIVITY

Chapter Summary:

Chapter 16 discusses impulsivity, a typical issue for teenagers as they traverse the complexity of decision-making and self-control. According to Icard, impulsivity may lead to unsafe actions and bad judgments, thus parents should assist their teenagers develop impulse management methods. The chapter highlights the need of teaching self-regulation skills, such as stopping before making judgments and evaluating the possible implications of their actions. Icard urges parents to have open talks about the effect of impulsivity in their life and to collaborate on ways for making informed choices. Parents may assist their teenagers make more thoughtful and studied decisions by encouraging self-awareness and offering impulse control tools.

Key Takeaways:

- Impulsivity may lead to unsafe actions and bad judgments, therefore it's critical to educate kids how to manage their impulses.

- Self-regulation skills, such as stopping and pondering the implications, are critical for making informed choices.

- Open talks about how impulsivity affects everyday living help teenagers grasp the value of self-control.

- Teens may improve their decision-making abilities by learning to detect triggers for impulsive conduct.

- Giving teenagers skills and tactics for impulse control, such as mindfulness or reflective practices, helps them make more thoughtful decisions.

- Parents should serve as role models for self-regulation and careful decision-making, teaching how to successfully manage urges.

- Encouraging teenagers to think on previous hasty acts and their consequences may lead to increased self-awareness and improved decision-making in the future.

Self-Reflection Questions:

How do you now assist your adolescent control impulsive behaviors and make better informed decisions?

_____

_____

_____

_____

_____

_____

Are you modeling self-regulation and impulse control in your own life, and how does this affect your teenager?

_____

_____

_____

_____

_____

_____

How can you help your adolescent identify triggers for impulsive behavior and create skills to control them?

_____

_____

_____

_____

_____

_____

How can you foster open talks about how impulsivity affects your teen's life and decisions?

_____

_____

_____

_____

_____

_____

Do you provide your adolescent skills and tactics for impulse management, such as mindfulness or reflective practices?

_____

_____

_____

_____

_____

_____

How can you assist your adolescent learn from prior hasty acts and apply those lessons to make better judgments in the future?

_____

_____

_____

_____

_____

_____

Life-Changing Exercises:

Practice "pause and reflect" activities with your adolescent, in which they ponder for a minute before making a choice and explore the possible repercussions.

Role-play situations in which your adolescent must exercise impulse control while leading them through the process of making a sensible decision.

Encourage your adolescent to create a notebook in which they chronicle impulsive choices and their consequences, commenting on trends and ideas for change.

Plan a family conversation about frequent triggers for impulsive behavior and suggest solutions for dealing with them.

Introduce mindfulness or relaxation practices to assist your adolescent manage stress and impulsivity, and practice them together.

Create a "decision-making toolkit" with your adolescent, which should include tactics for stopping, pondering, and weighing implications before taking action.

Encourage your adolescent to create personal objectives for developing impulse control, and monitor their progress together, celebrating victories and addressing obstacles.

Discuss with your adolescent instances of impulsive actions taken by prominent or historical people, including the consequences and lessons gained.

CHAPTER 17: TALKING ABOUT HELPING OTHERS

Chapter Summary:

Chapter 17 emphasizes the value of assisting others and developing compassion and social responsibility in youth. Icard highlights that volunteering and acts of kindness may have a significant influence on both the donor and the recipient, boosting personal development and community involvement. The chapter encourages parents to include their teenagers in activities that benefit others, such as community service, charity work, or helping friends and family. Icard emphasizes the advantages of helping others, such as enhanced empathy, a feeling of purpose, and better mental health. Parents may assist their teenagers develop a lifetime commitment to make a good impact in the world by modeling altruistic conduct and offering chances for them to participate.

Key Takeaways:

- Helping others fosters compassion, social responsibility, and personal development, which benefits both the giver and the recipient.

- Involving kids in volunteer activities or acts of kindness gives them a feeling of purpose and connection to their community.

- Acts of service may enhance mental health, boost empathy, and foster a good self-image.

- Parents should demonstrate altruistic conduct and encourage their children to engage in activities that benefit others.

- Providing chances for kids to participate in community service helps them realize how their actions affect others.

- Discussing the importance of assisting others and reflecting on their experiences might strengthen a teen's commitment to social responsibility.

- Helping others should be a meaningful and joyful activity, not a duty, in order to foster continued participation and compassion.

Self-Reflection Questions:

How do you now teach your adolescent about helping others

and taking on social responsibility?

_____

_____

_____

_____

_____

_____

Are you giving your adolescent opportunity to participate in

acts of service or community involvement?

_____

_____

_____

_____

_____

_____

How can you inspire your adolescent to discover personal fulfillment and pleasure in helping others?

_____

_____

_____

_____

_____

_____

How can you assist your adolescent reflect on their volunteering or acts of kindness?

_____

_____

_____

_____

_____

_____

How can you help your kid establish a long-term commitment to social duty and compassion?

_____

_____

_____

_____

_____

_____

How does your personal approach to assisting others impact your teen's views and behaviors?

_____

_____

_____

_____

_____

_____

Life-Changing Exercises:

Volunteer as a family at a local group, discussing the effect of your efforts and commenting on your experiences.

Encourage your kid to select a cause that they are passionate about and create a project or event to promote it, coaching them along the way.

Discuss with your child how they might assist others, whether via tiny acts of kindness or major community service programs.

Create a "kindness challenge" in which each family member commits to doing a specified number of acts of kindness over the course of a week and then shares their experiences.

Encourage your adolescent to think about a moment when they helped someone and how it made them feel, examining the personal effect of their actions.

Invite a guest speaker from a charitable group to highlight the significance of helping others and provide volunteer opportunities.

Encourage your adolescent to create a "service journal" in which they may document their volunteer experiences, personal observations, and the results of their work.

Discuss the notion of social responsibility and how it links to your family's beliefs, and look for ways to integrate it into your everyday life.

SELF-EVALUATION QUESTIONS

How well do I communicate with my adolescent about the subjects discussed in the book, and how can I enhance these conversations?

_____

_____

_____

_____

_____

How have I changed my communication style to better connect with my adolescent, and what other tactics may I try?

_____

_____

_____

_____

_____

_____

How successfully do I model the behaviors and values I want my adolescent to learn, and what adjustments can I make to better match my actions with my teachings?

_____

_____

_____

_____

_____

How open am I to addressing difficult things with my adolescent, and what can I do to make these talks more comfortable?

_____

_____

_____

_____

_____

Have I effectively given my kid the skills and methods he or she needs to deal with problems like criticism, hard work, and impulsivity? If not, what measures can I take to resolve this?

_____

_____

_____

_____

_____

How efficiently can I assist my kid in managing their relationships, independence, and reputation, and what further assistance could they need in these areas?

_____

_____

_____

_____

_____

_____

What have been the most difficult problems in talking themes such as sexuality and money with my teenager, and how can I handle them more effectively?

_____

_____

_____

_____

_____

_____

How can I help my kid establish a strong work ethic and a good attitude toward hard work, and what changes can I make in this area?

_____

_____

_____

_____

_____

_____

How well do I understand my teen's viewpoints on problems like technology, creativity, and justice, and how can I better connect with them?

_____

_____

_____

_____

_____

_____

How can I inspire my adolescent to serve others and perform acts of kindness, and how can I strengthen their commitment to social responsibility?

_____

_____

_____

_____

_____

_____

How can I address my teen's impulsivity, and what tactics can I use to assist them build stronger self-control and decision-making abilities?

_____

_____

_____

_____

_____

How have I implemented lessons on managing criticism and feedback into our family dynamic, and what more steps can I take to reinforce these teachings?

_____

_____

_____

_____

_____

How can I strike a balance between offering direction and letting my adolescent to make their own choices, and how can I modify this balance to better support their development?

_____

_____

_____

_____

_____

What role do I have in molding my teen's perception of their own reputation and self-image, and how can I assist them develop a good and honest reputation?

_____

_____

_____

_____

How have our discussions about helping others affected my teen's conduct and views, and what more can I do to create a true sense of compassion and community involvement?

_____

_____

_____

_____

_____

_____

_____

_____

_____

_____

_____

Made in the USA
Columbia, SC
23 October 2024

44963375R00085